Under Water Watercolor

Scrap Book Paper

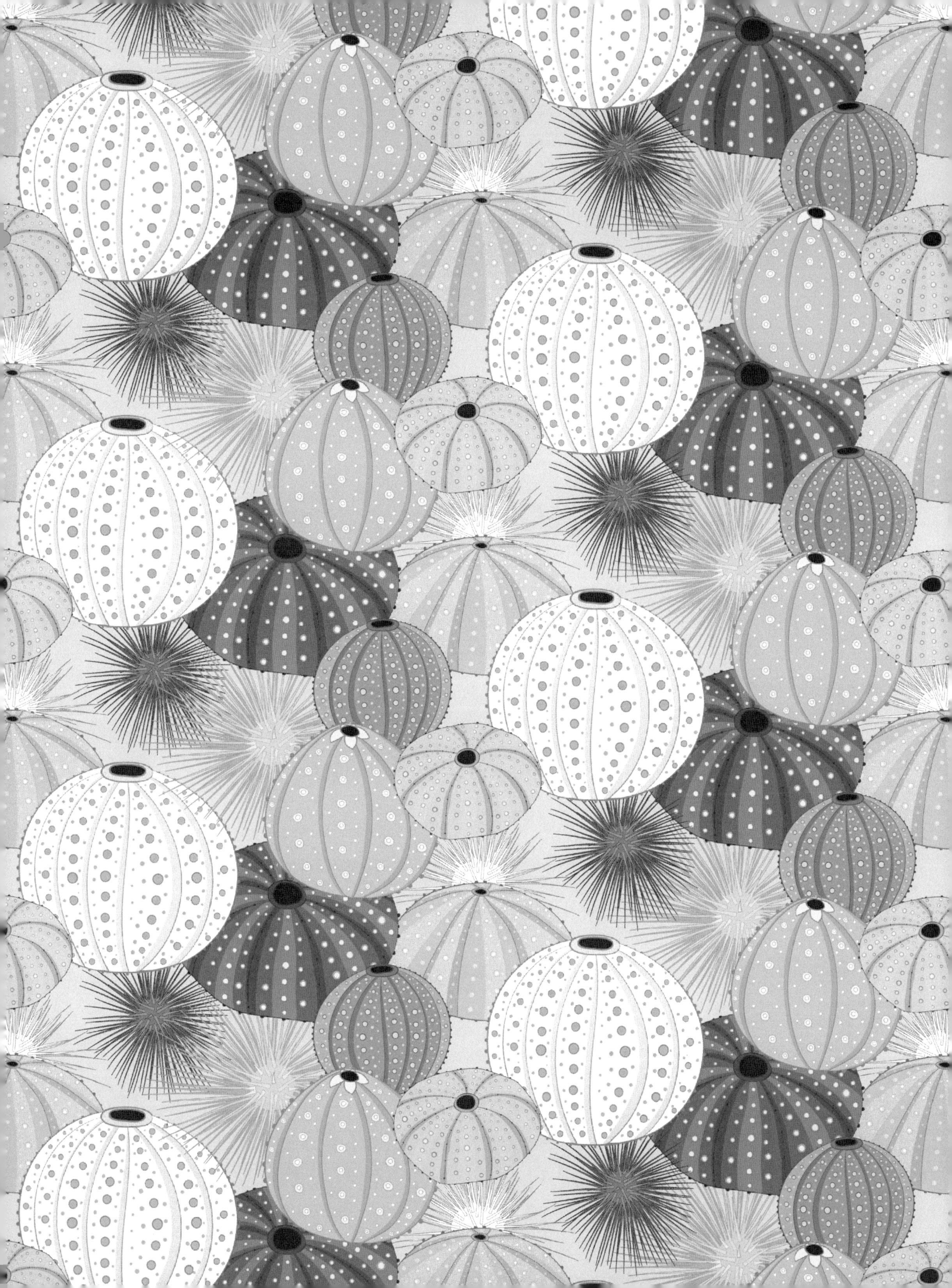

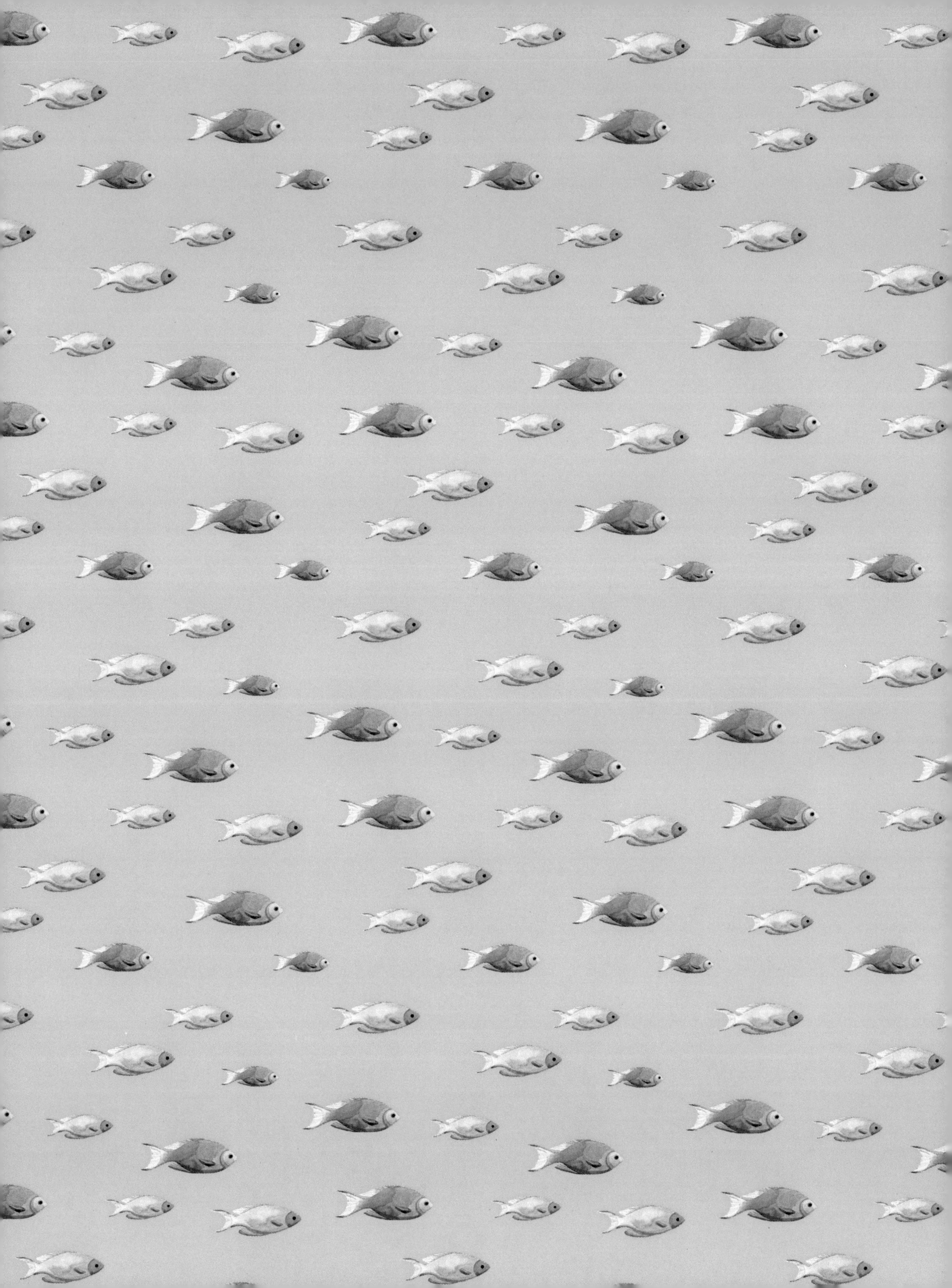

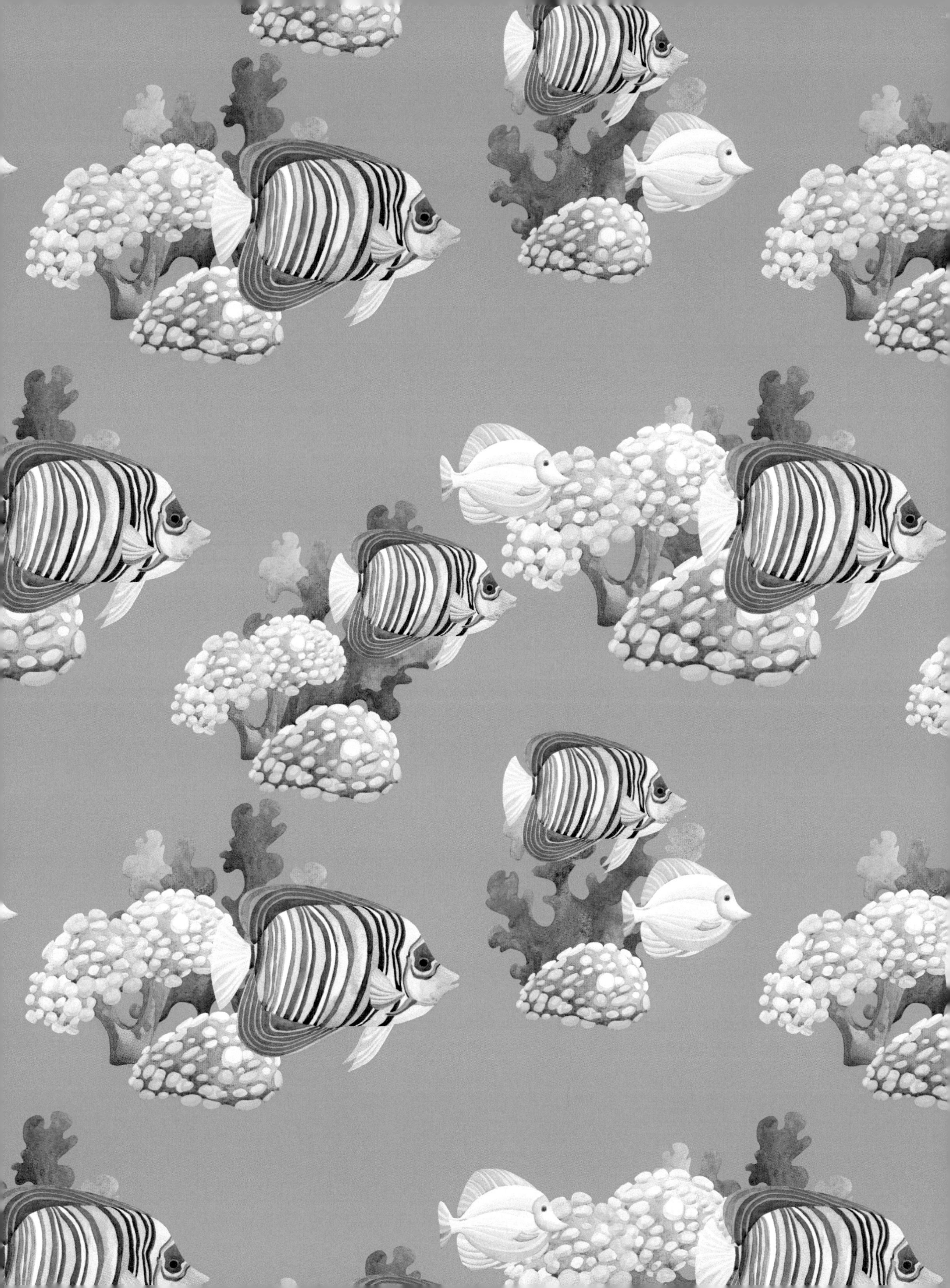

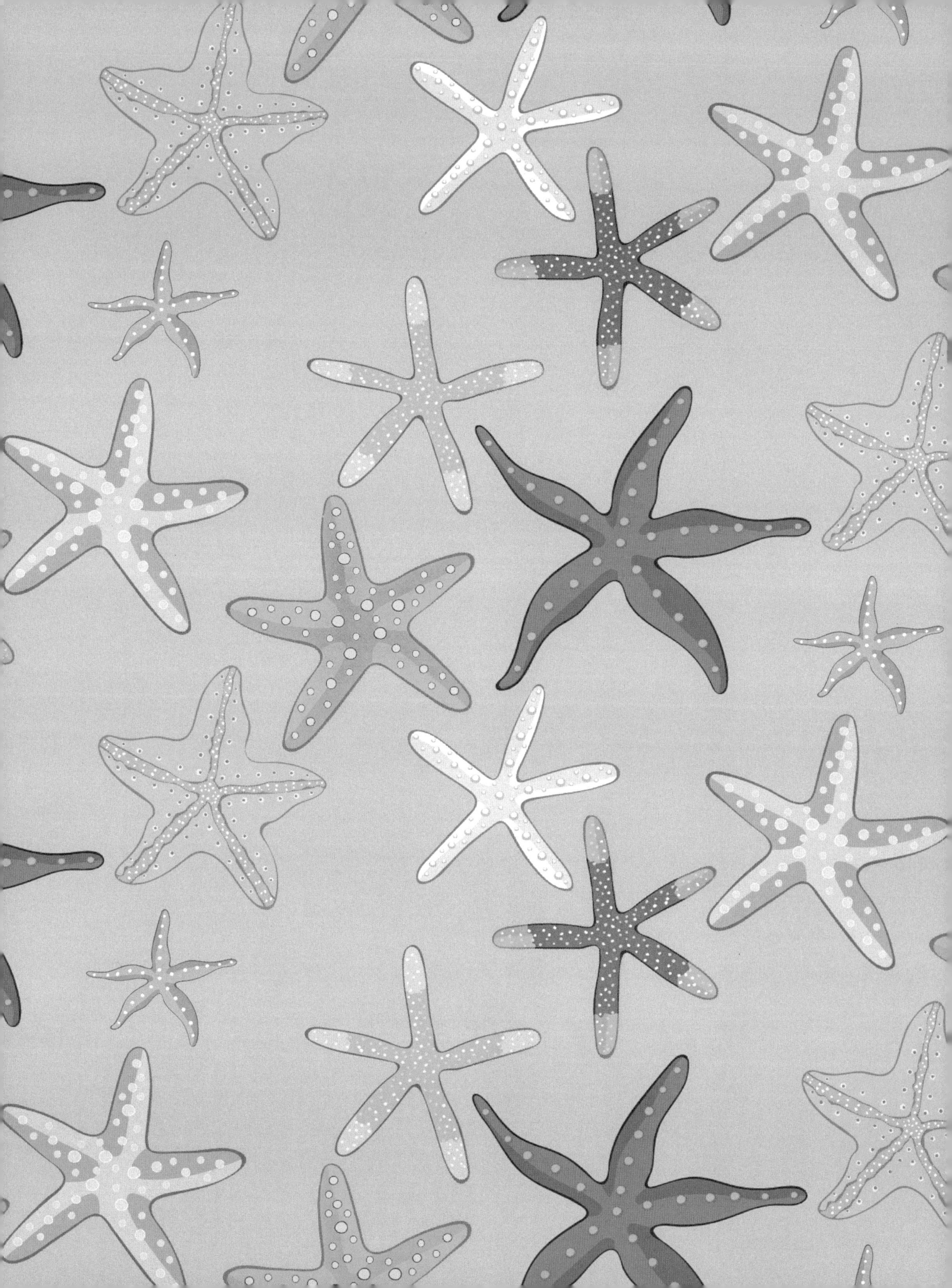

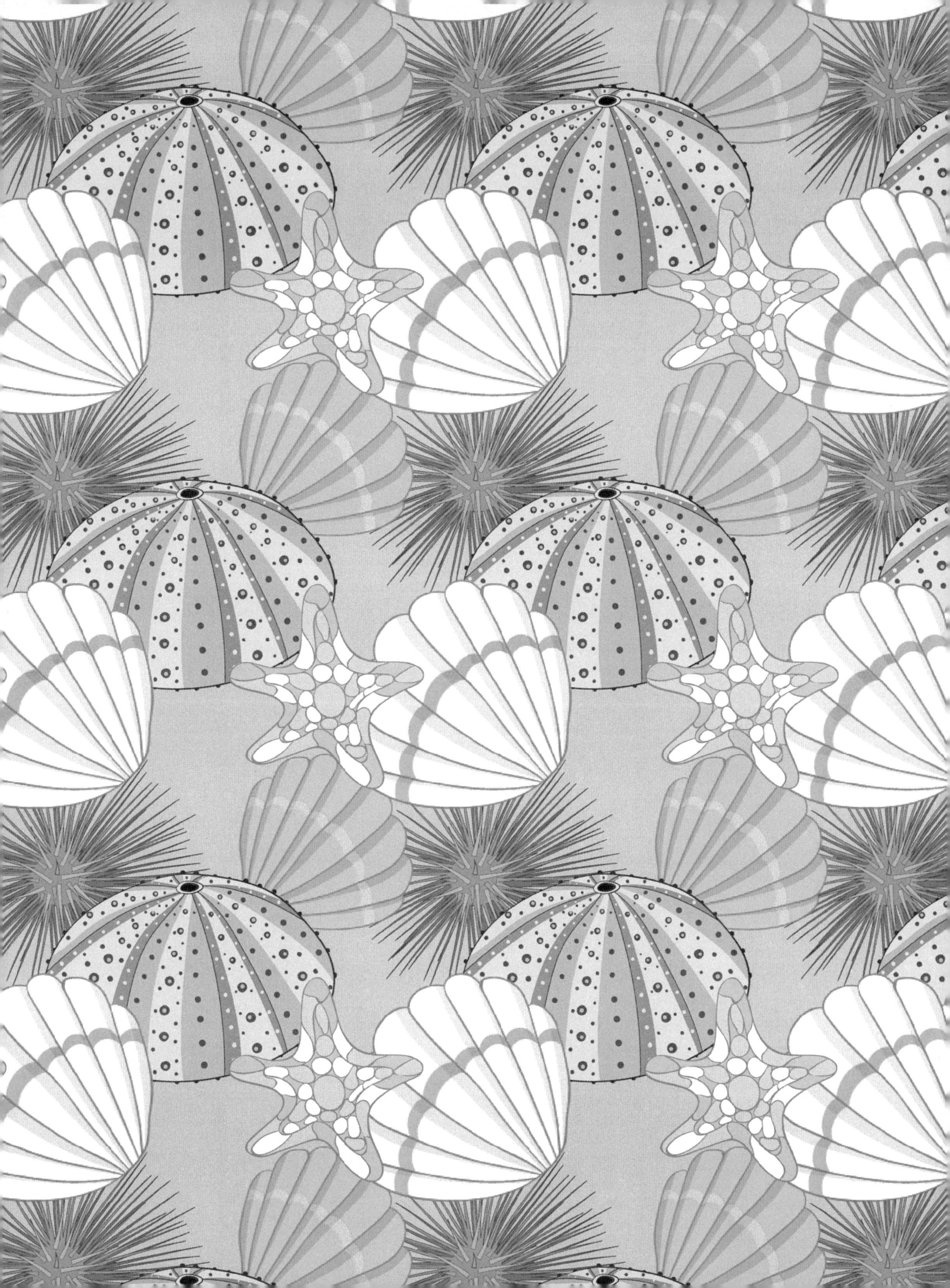

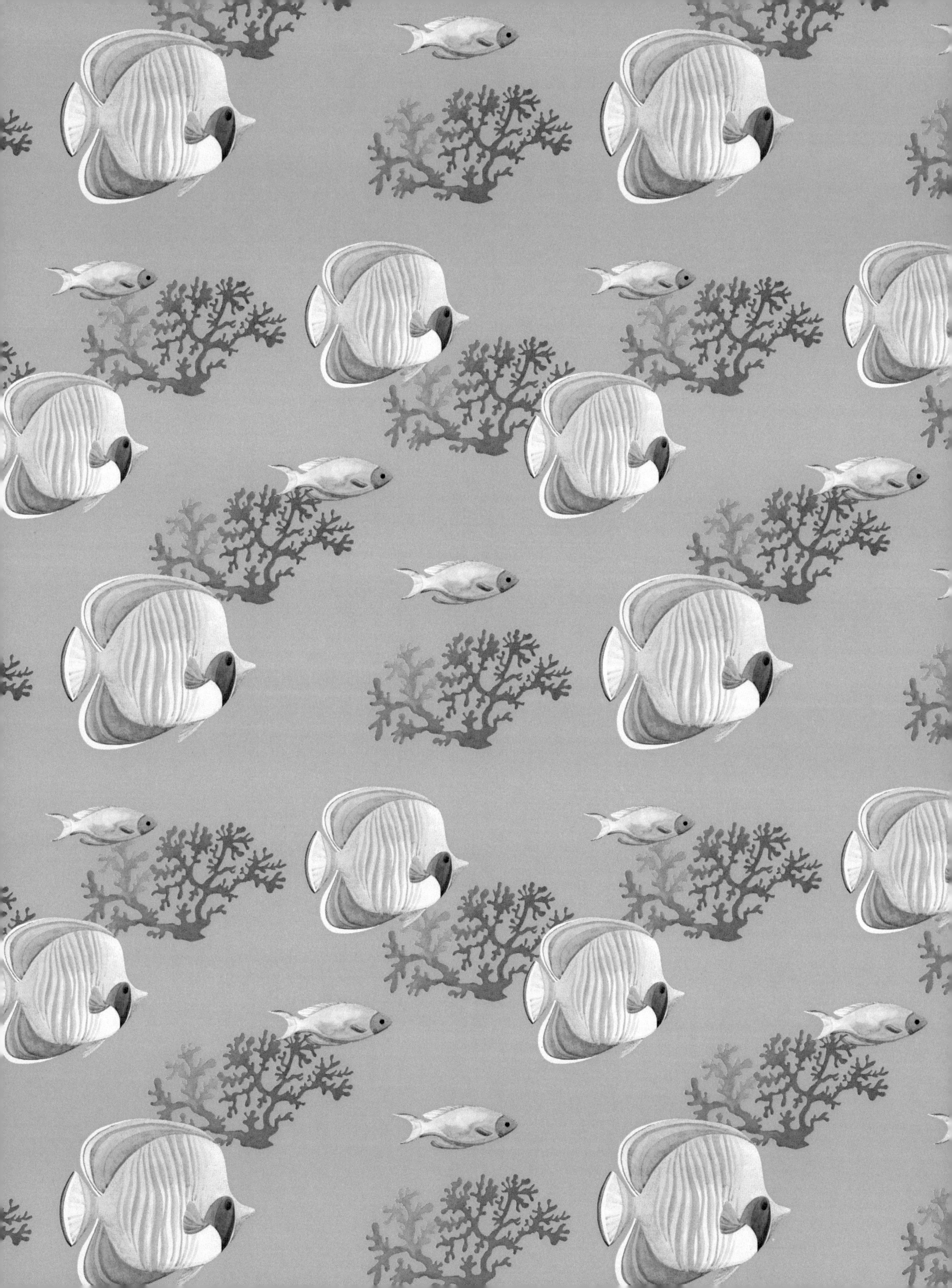

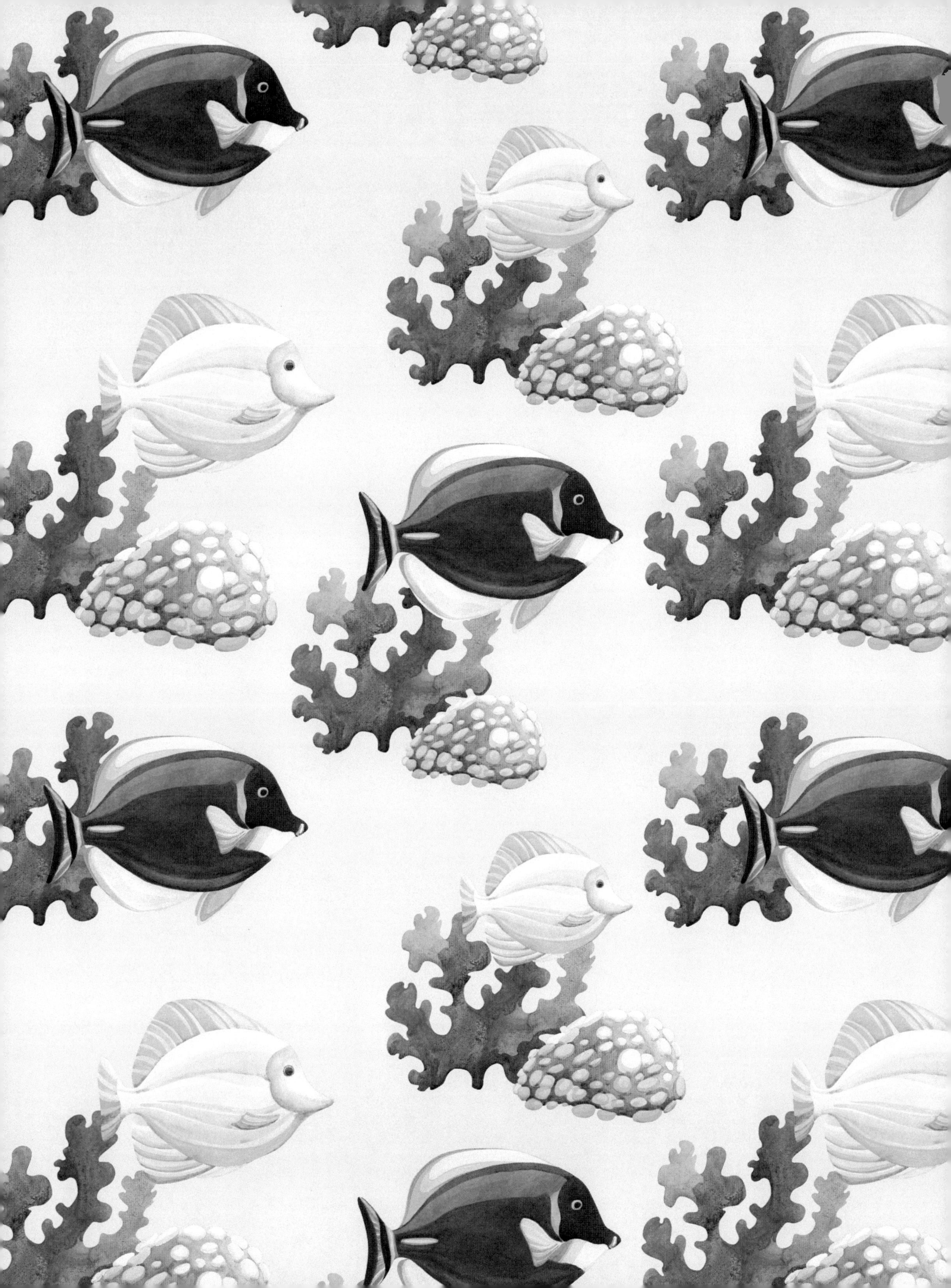

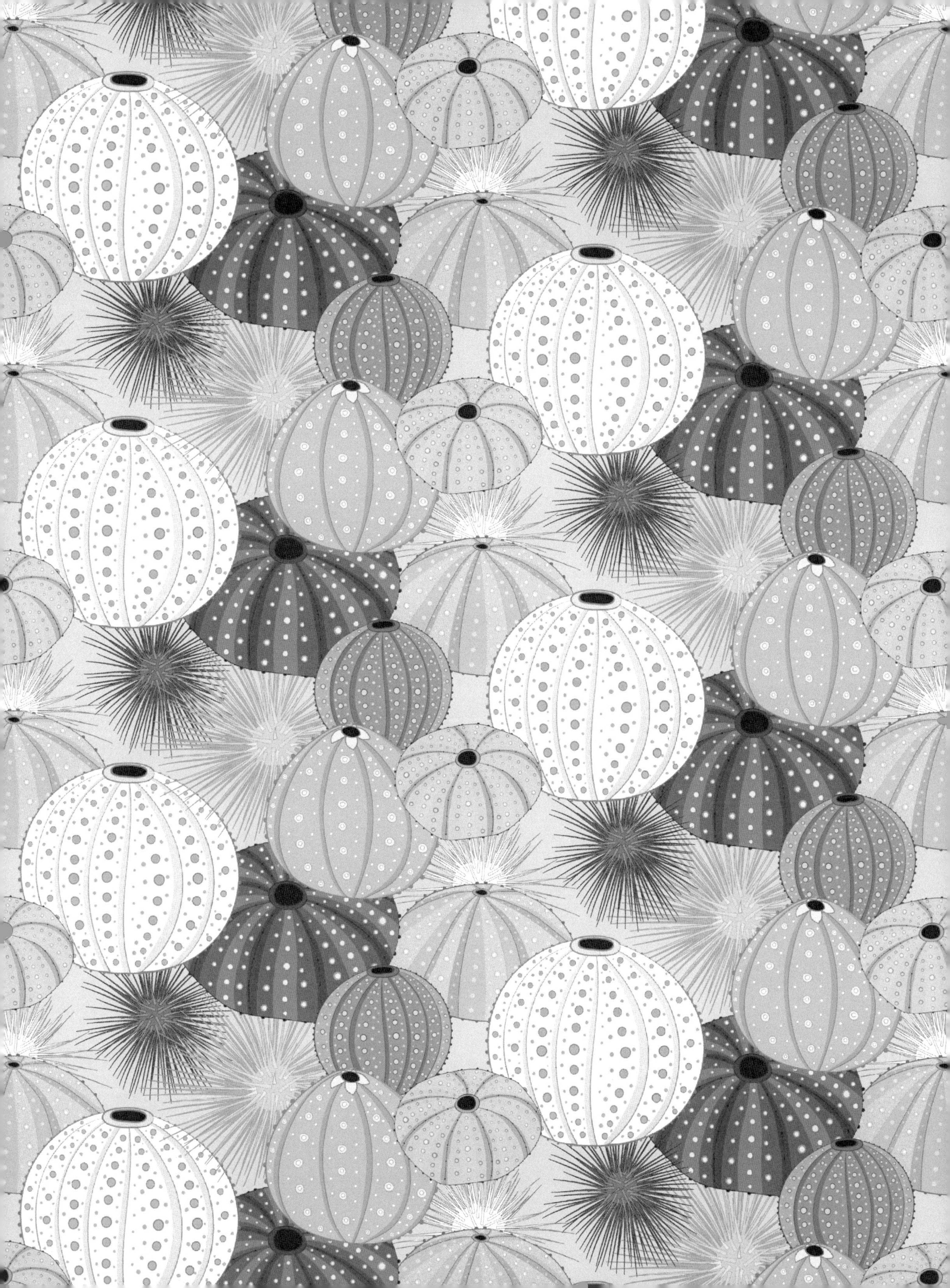

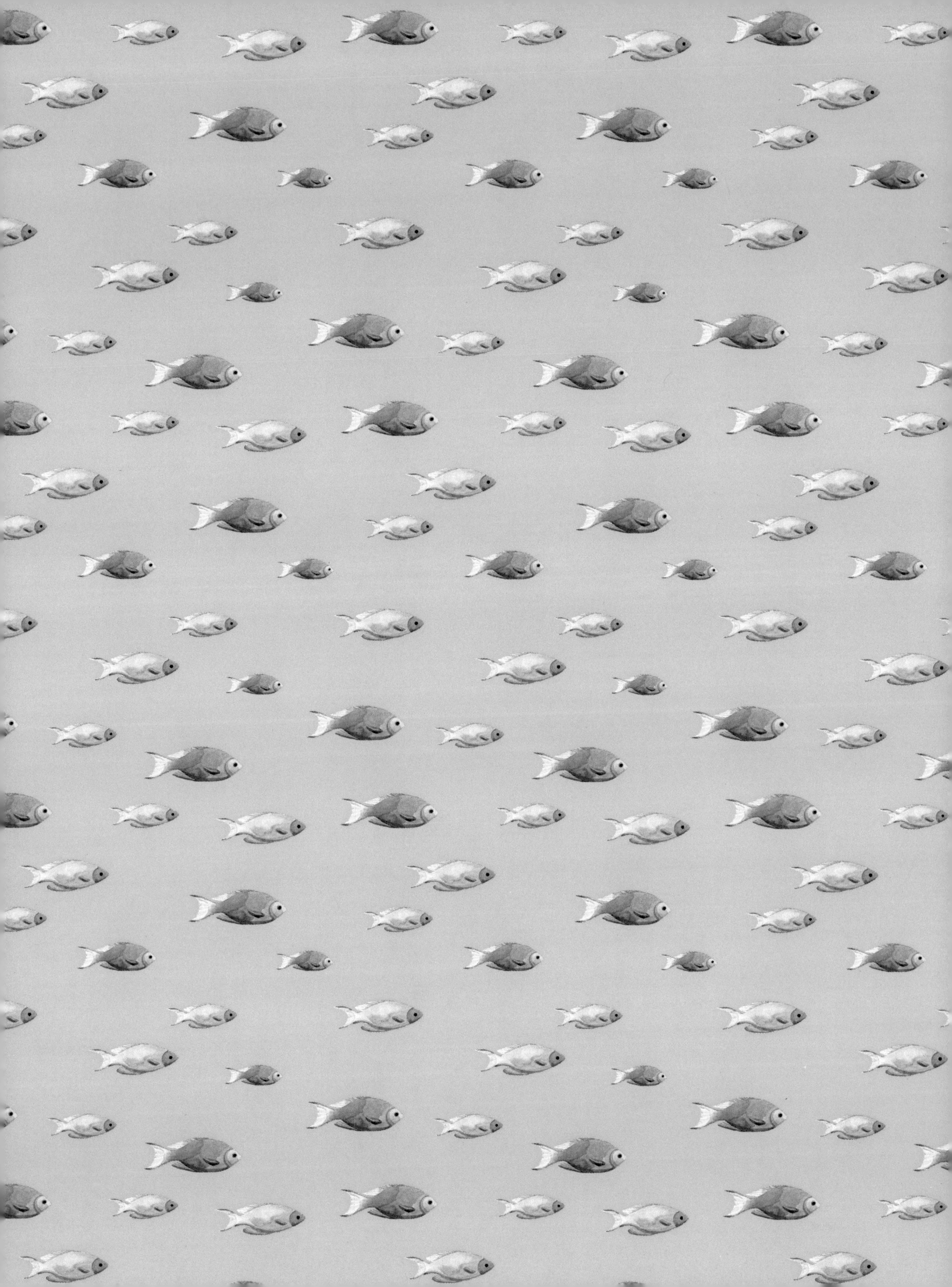

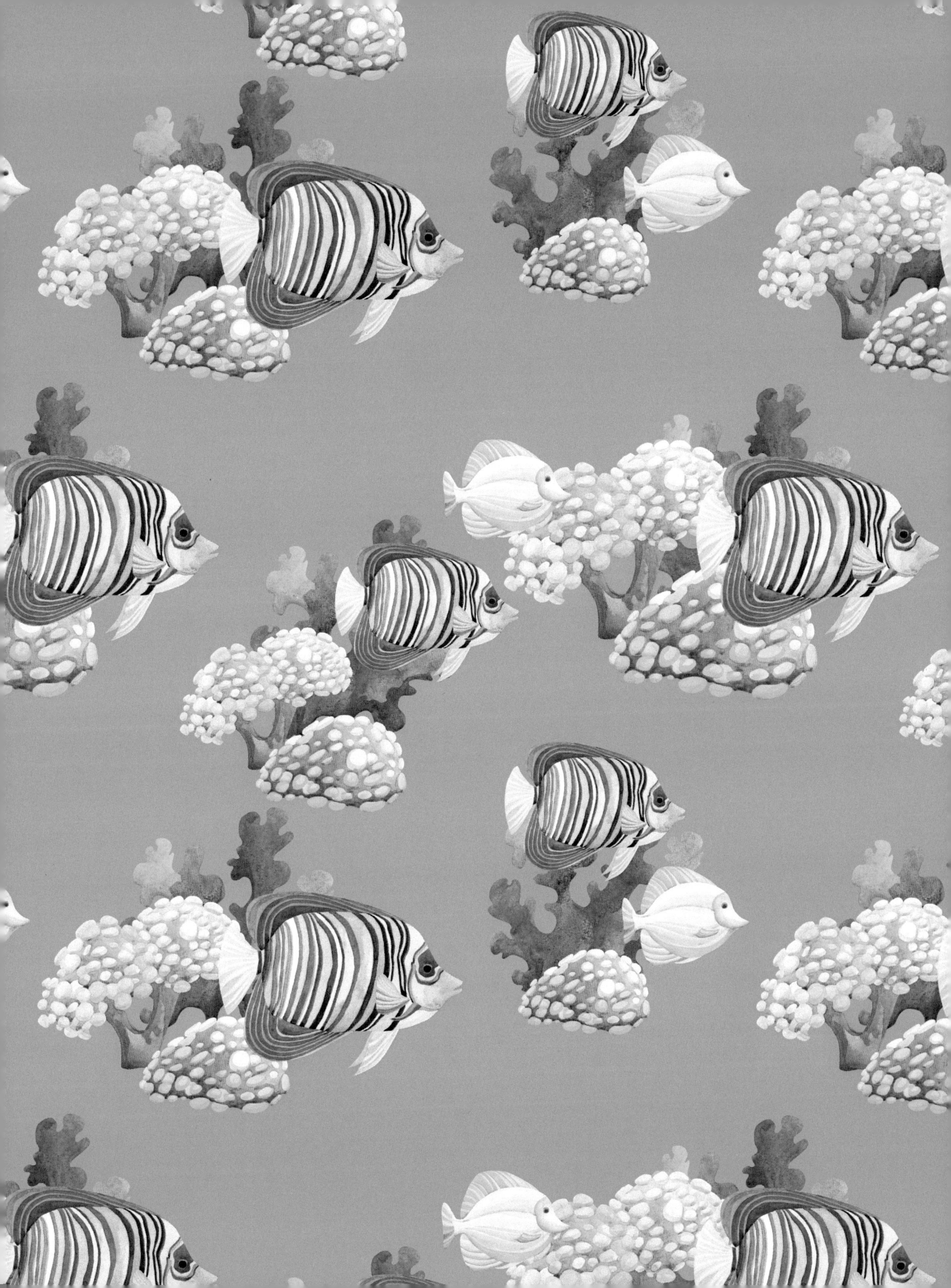

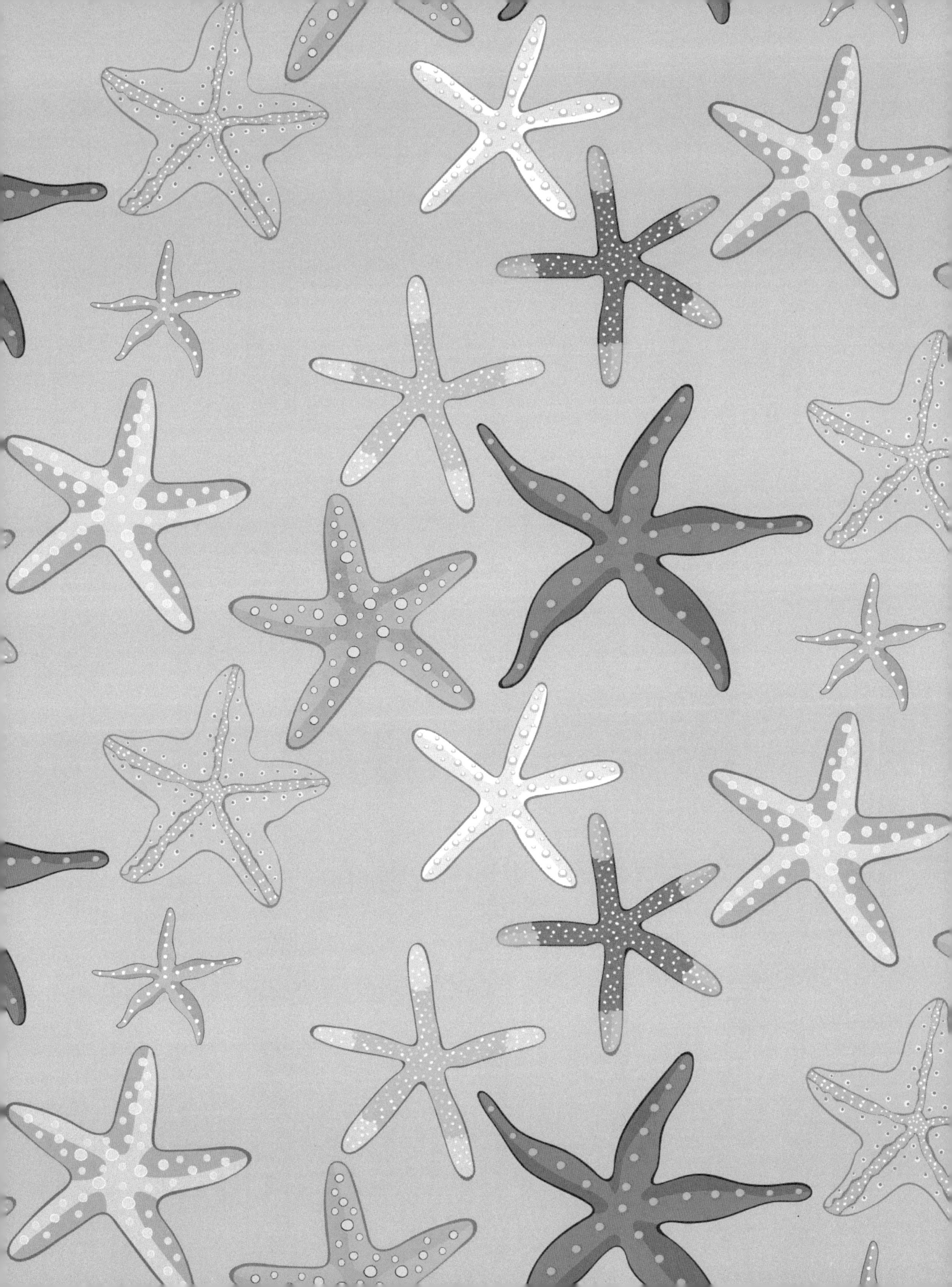

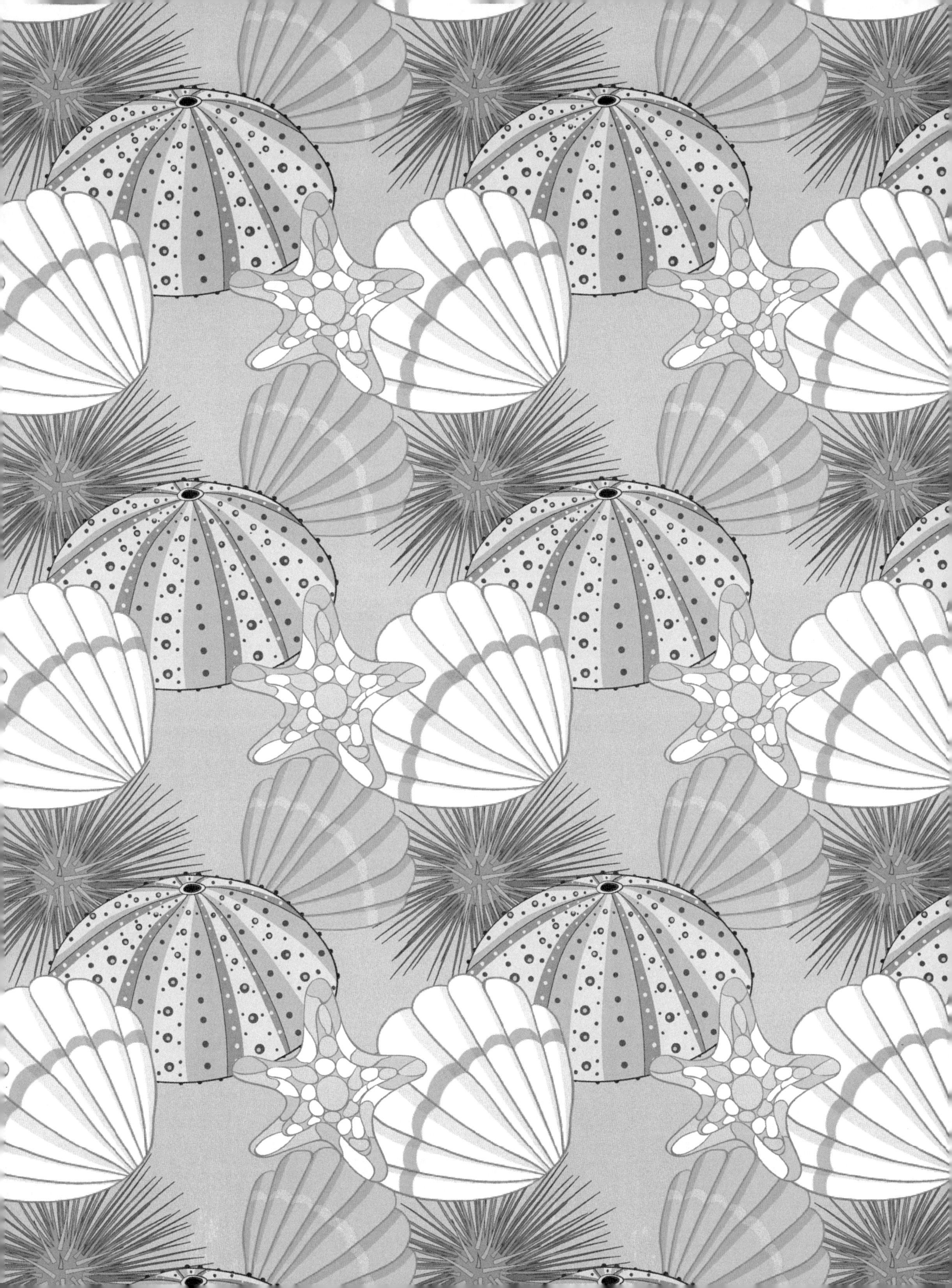

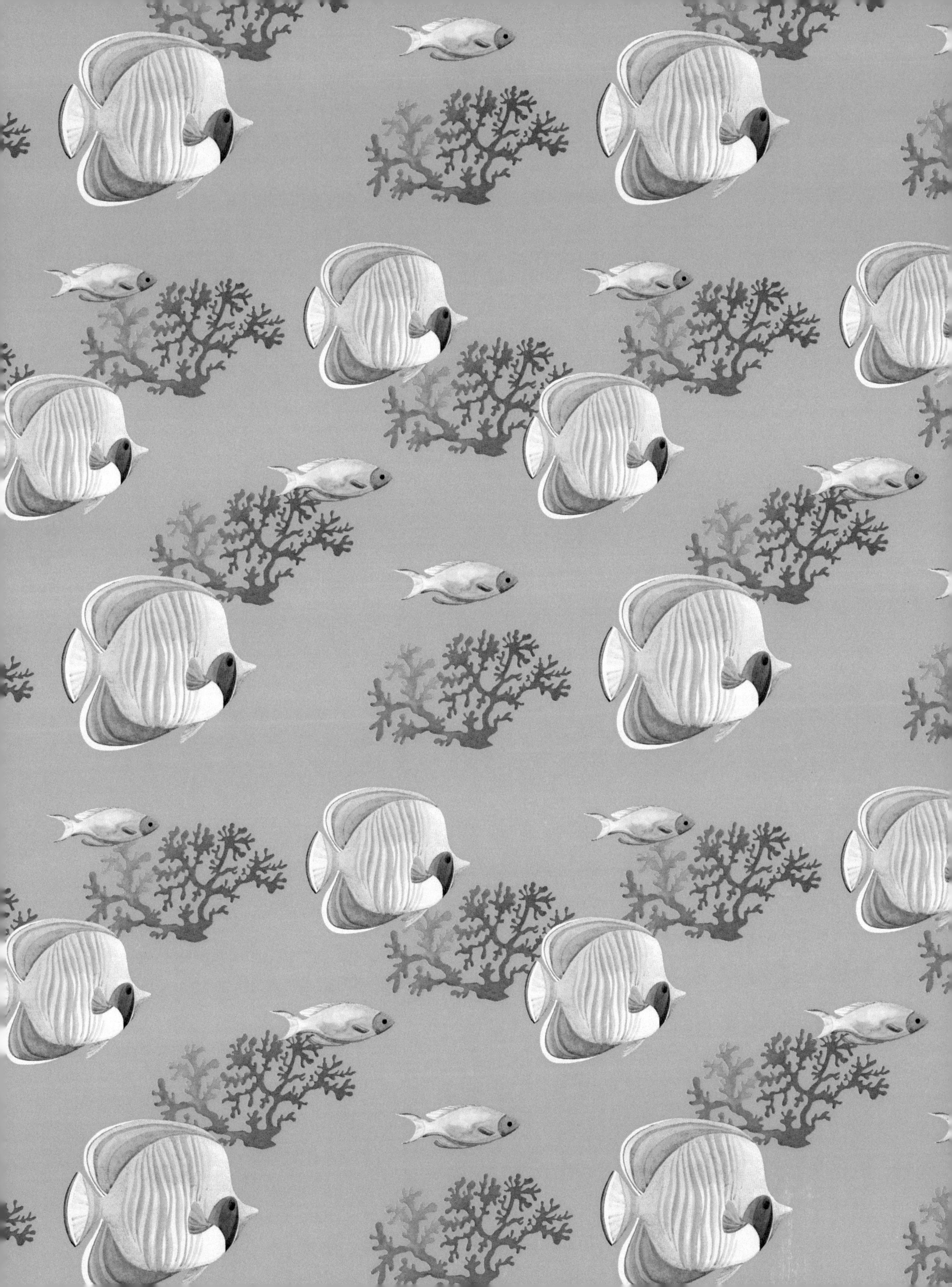

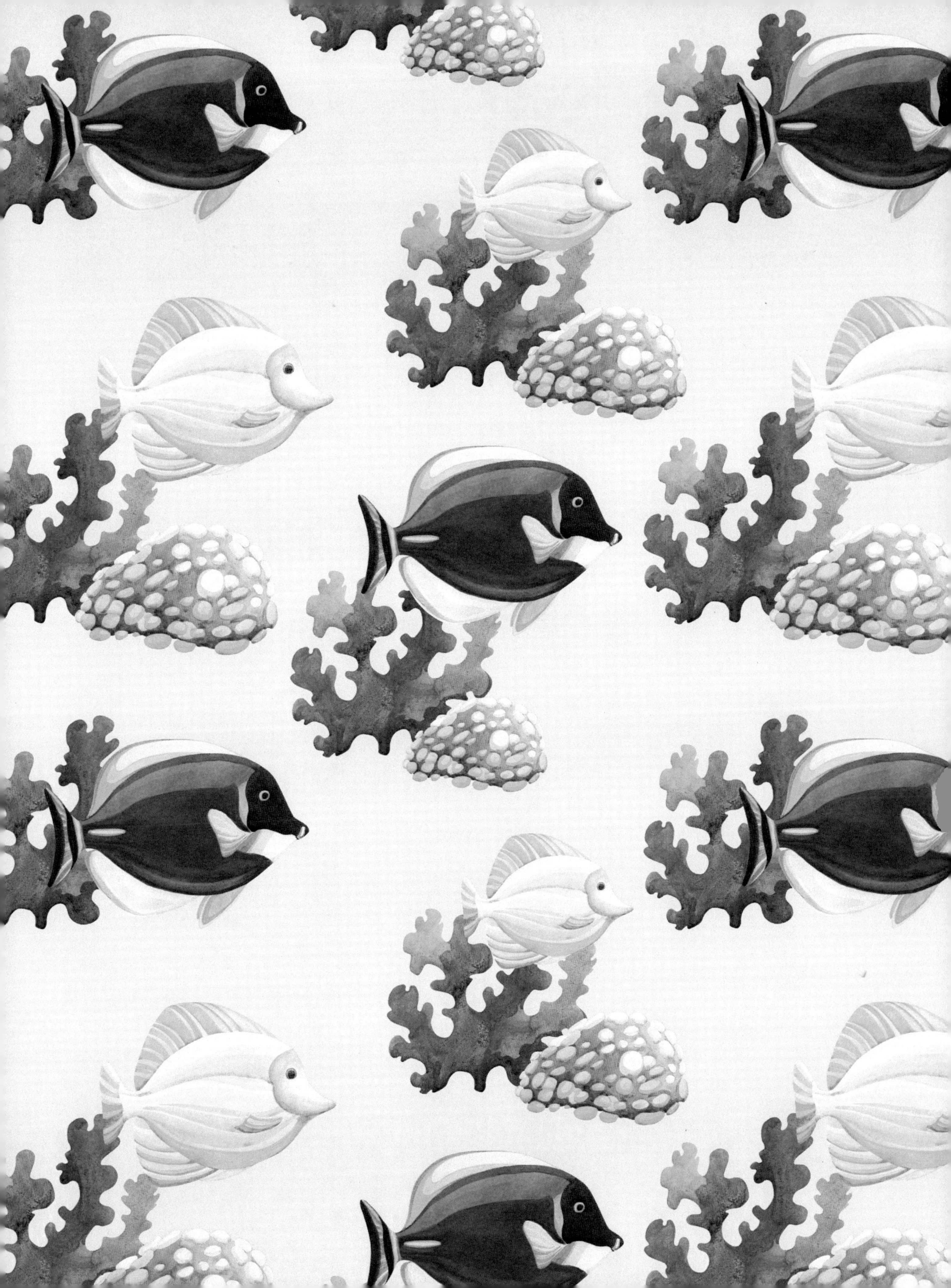

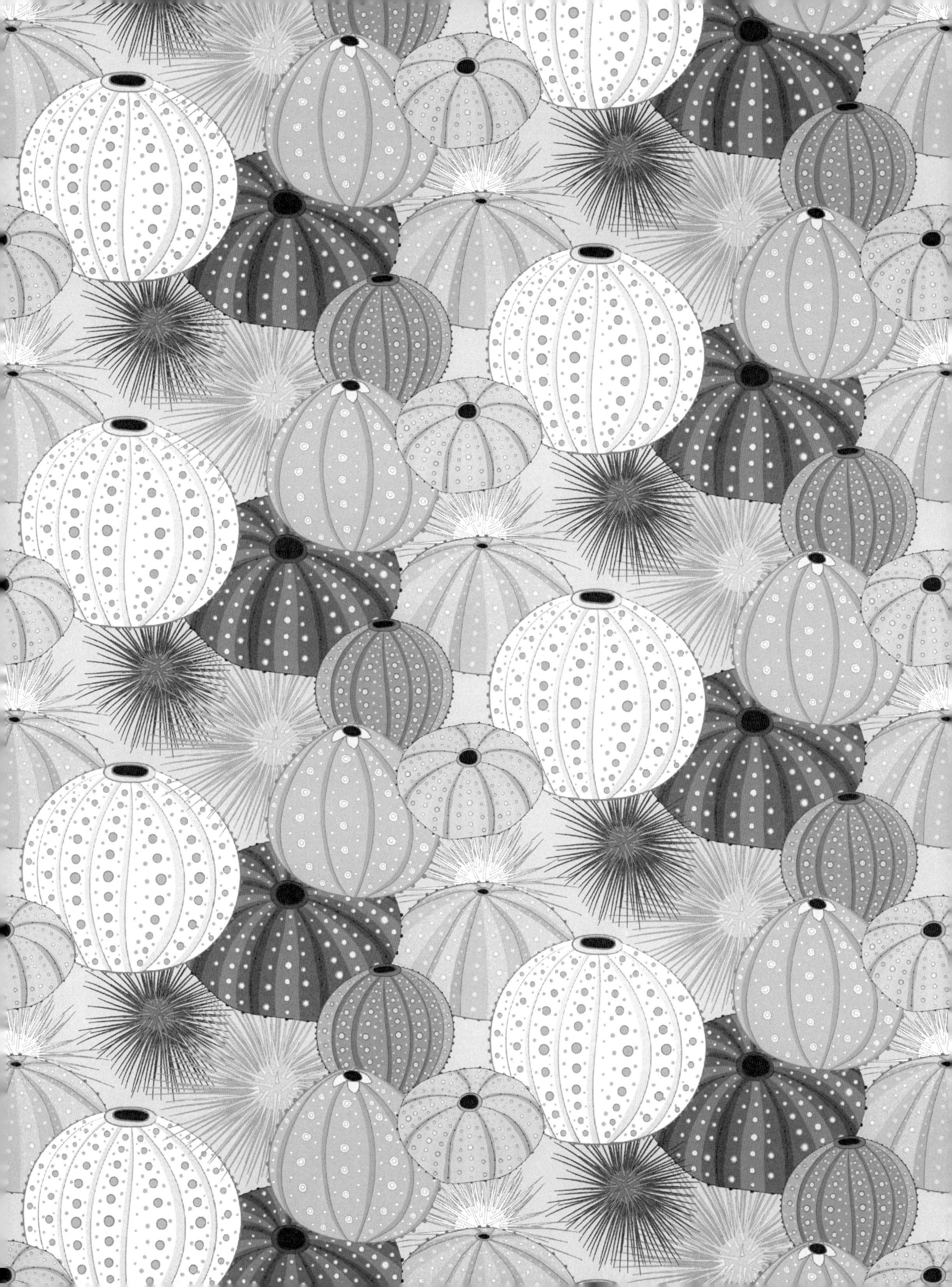

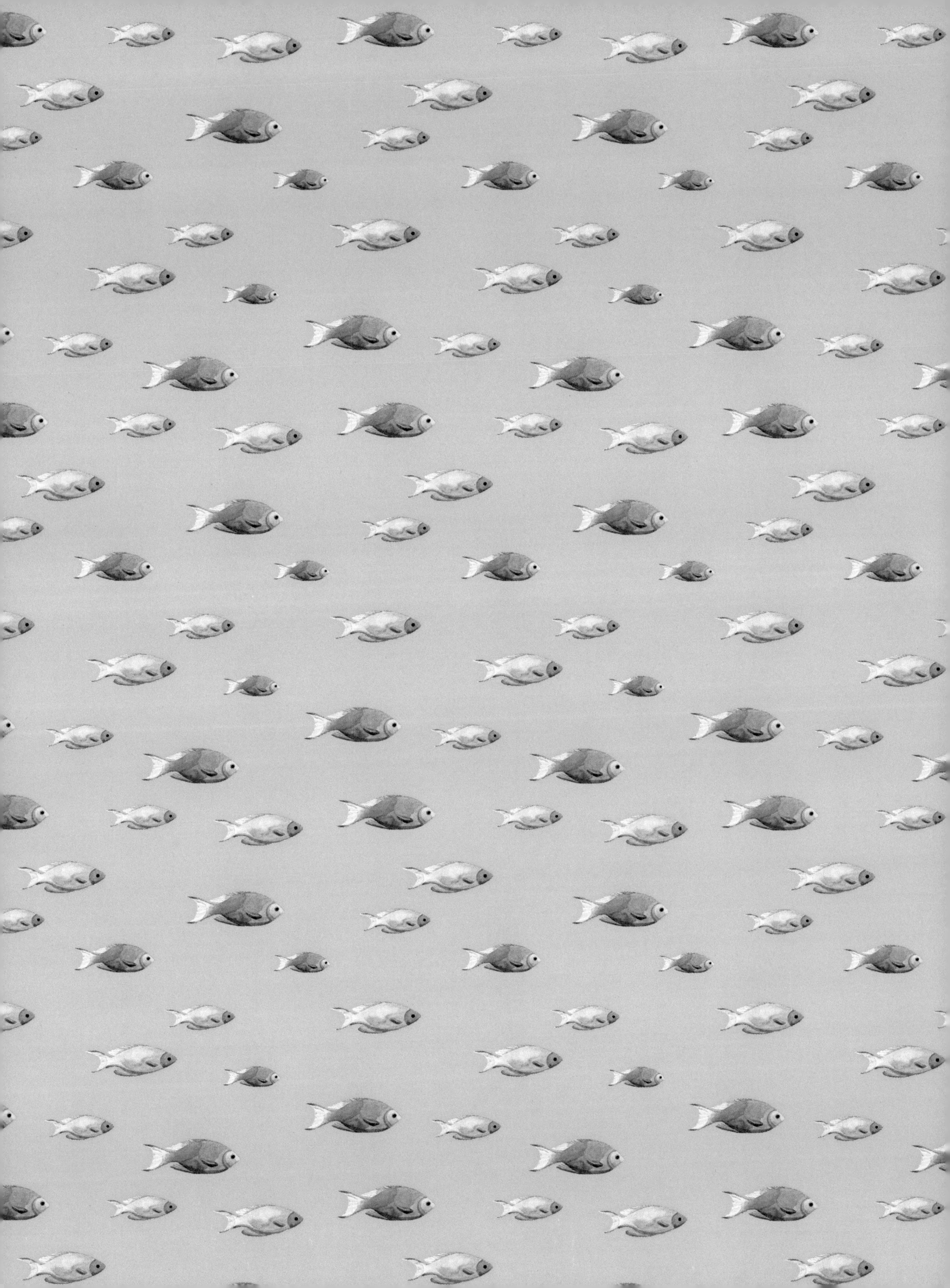

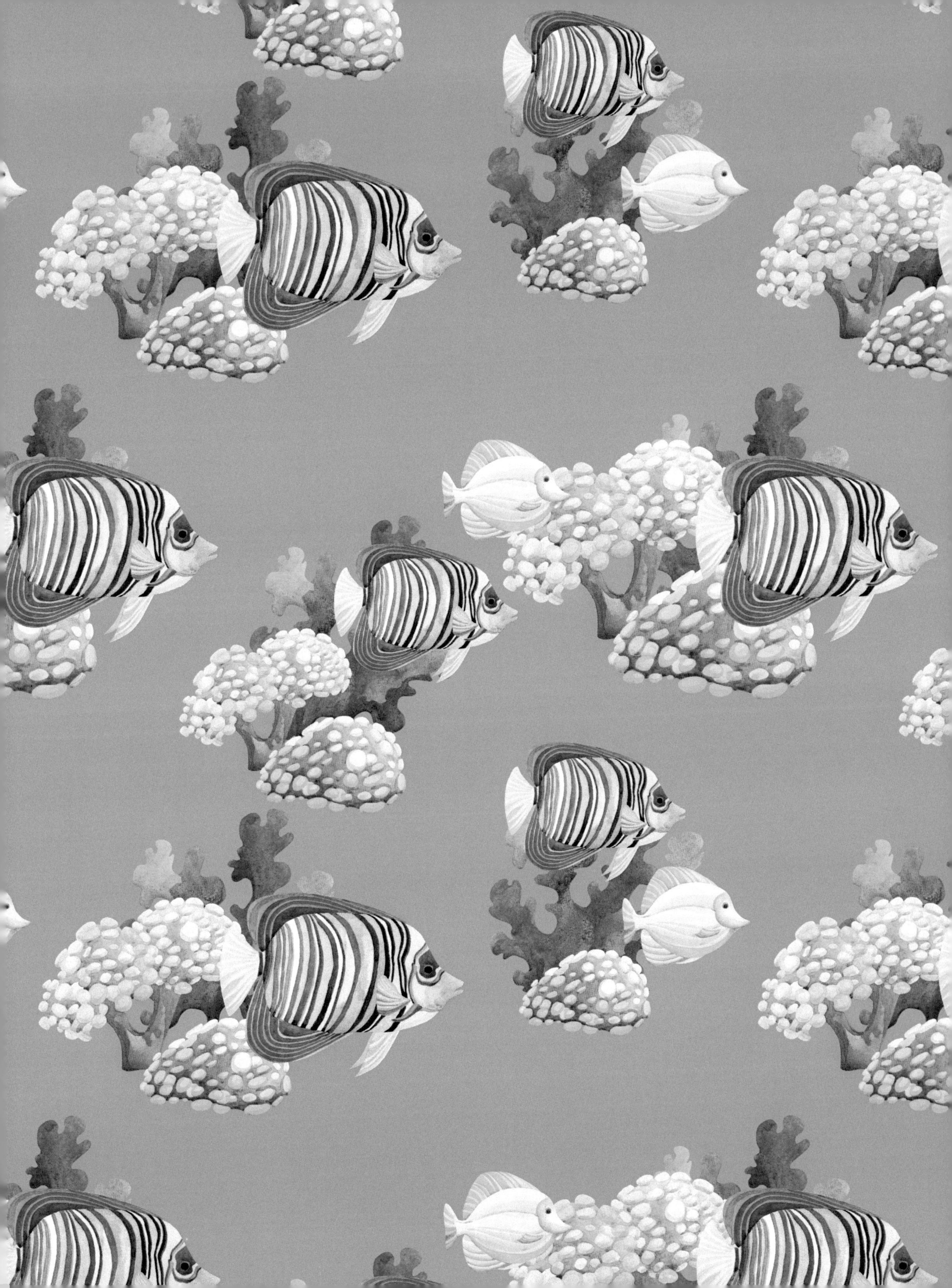

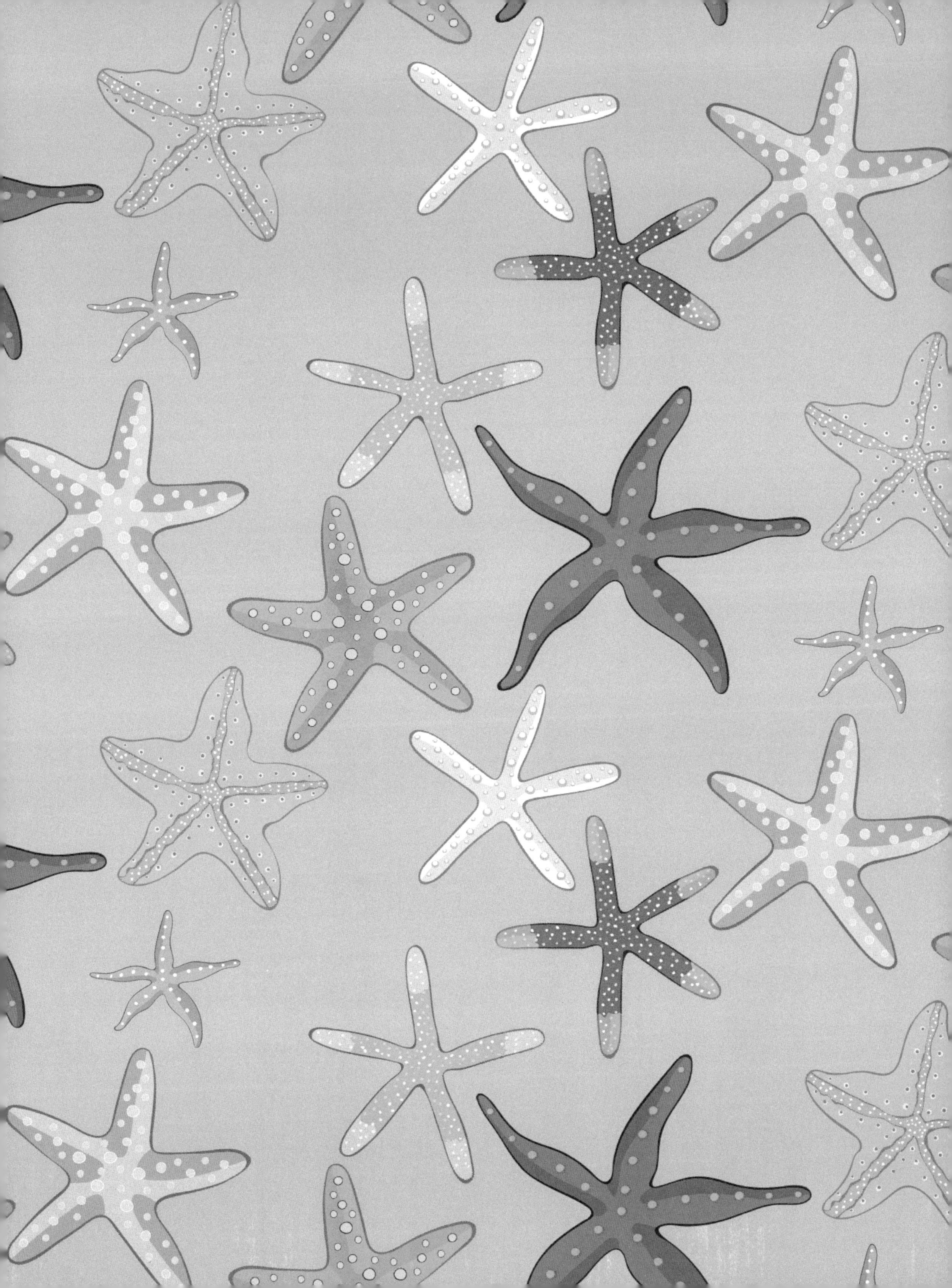

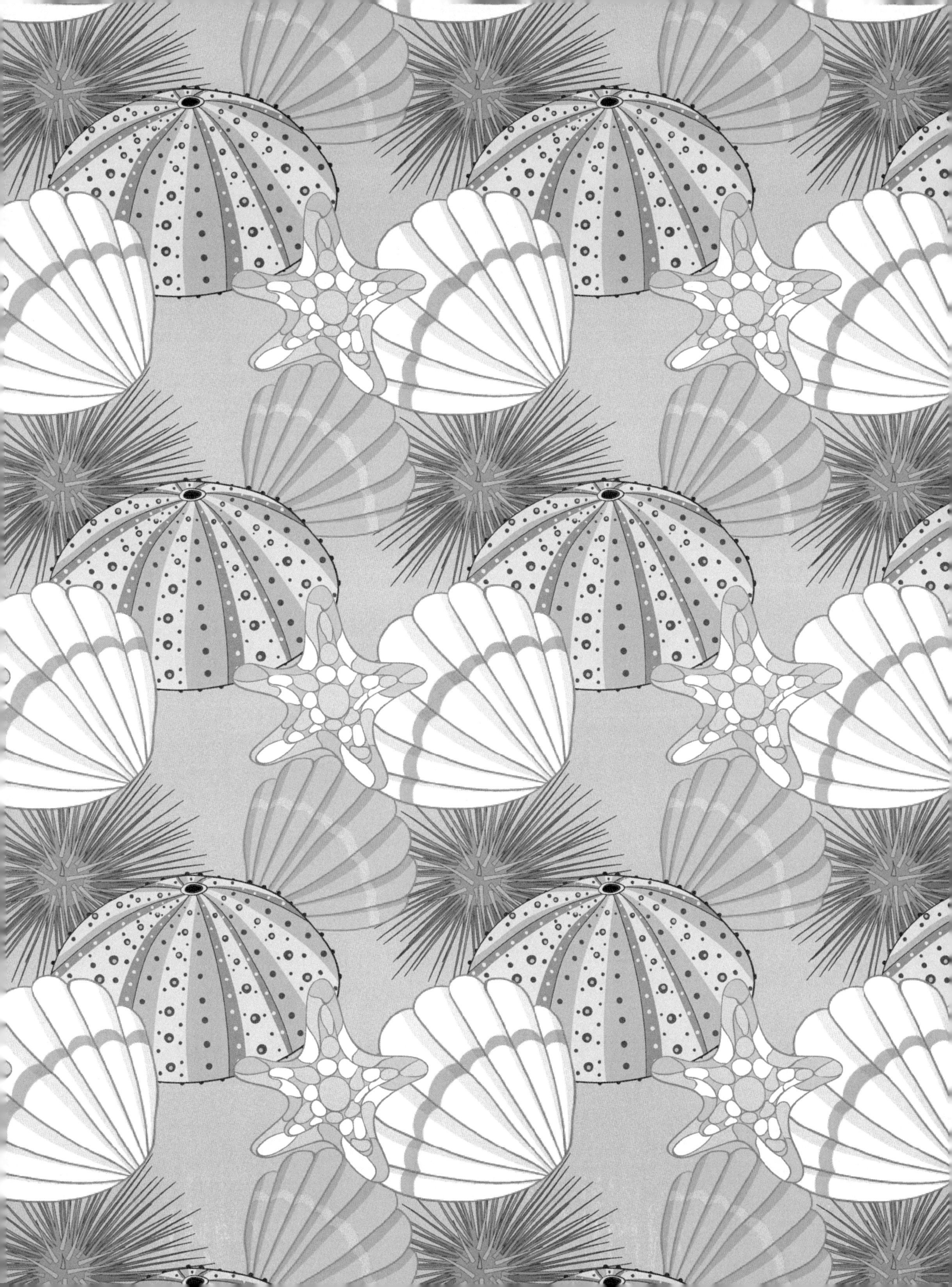

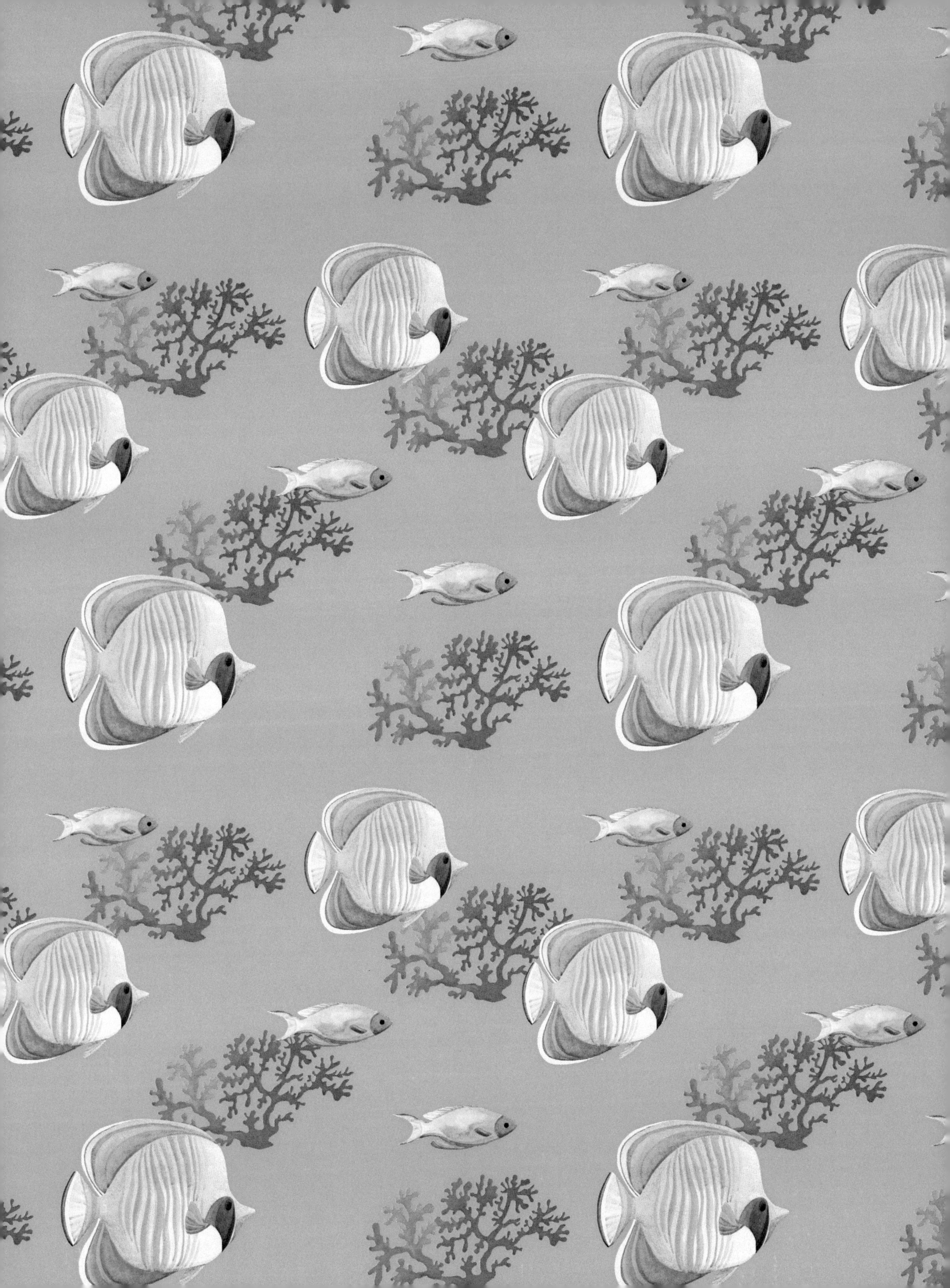

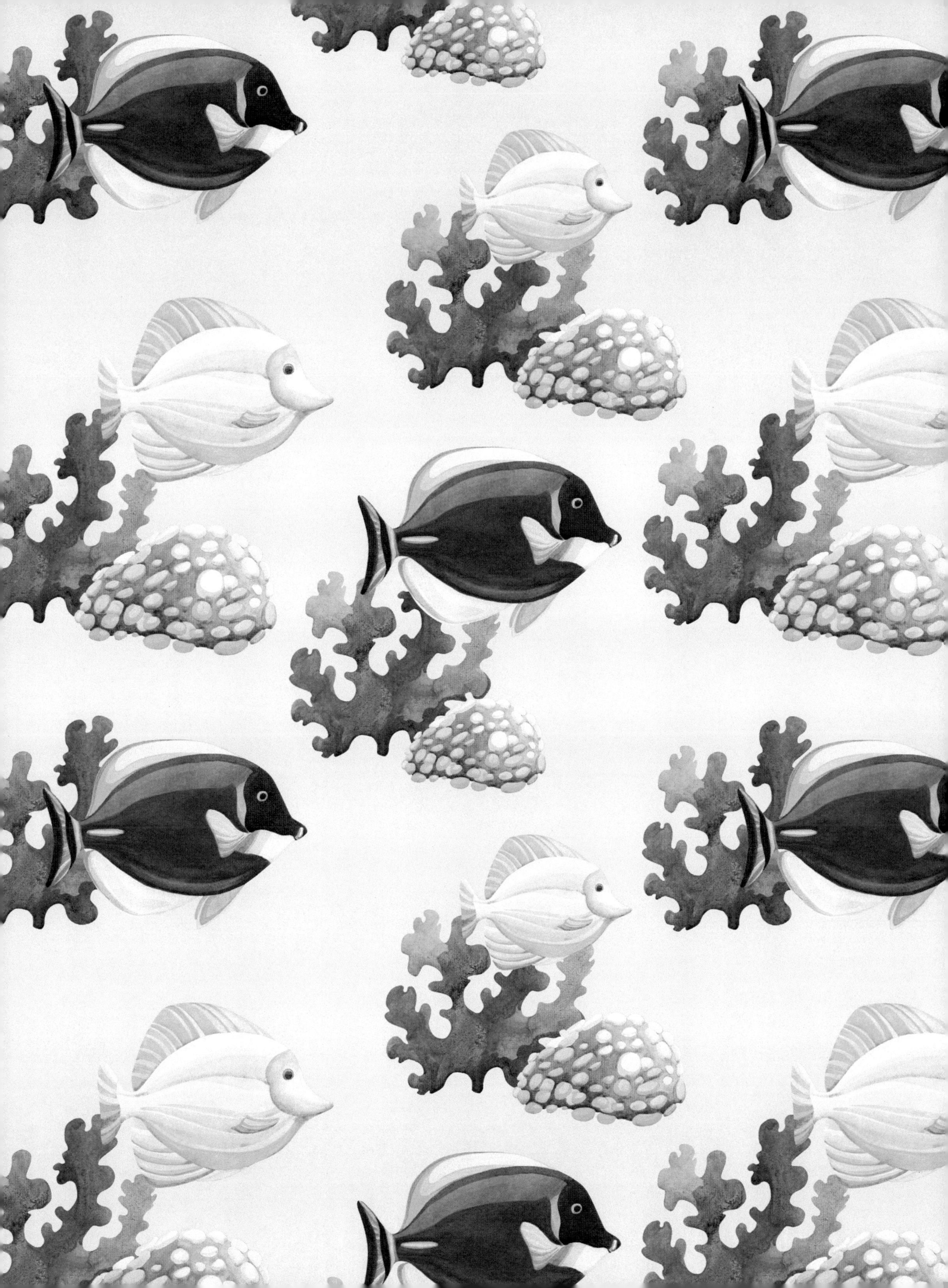